Listening *for* Success

How *to* Master

the

Most Important Skill

of

Network Marketing

By

STEVE SHAPIRO

Chica Publications

"For years I have taught distributors: "Magnetize, don't pulverize!" A successful MLM business begins with *attracting* good people into your organization and then caring enough to help them reach their goals. Nothing will make you more attractive to others than mastering the art of listening. It's the best way to show you really care and will help you build a successful life as well as a strong and loyal downline. Get this book into the hands of your distributors and create a team of powerfully magnetic personalities!"

Alon Sagee
Laguna Beach, CA

Table of Contents

Why Read this Book?

*"Listen carefully to my words;
let your ears take in what I say.*
-Job 13:17

LISTENING IS LIKE PICKING FRUIT FROM A TREE. Sometimes you get a bad piece of fruit. Sometimes mediocre, and sometimes you get the juiciest, ripest piece. But you only get to the good fruit by picking fruit. If you don't pick any fruit, you don't get bad fruit or good fruit. When you interrupt someone, finish their sentence, talk too much or respond too quickly, it's like stomping on the tree before it's even had a chance to produce fruit. However, if you listen to someone and try your hardest to understand who they are, they will eventually produce ripe fruit for you. Some of what they say may be irrelevant, incorrect, or misguided—like rotten fruit. But some of it may give you the key to what motivates and inspires them to take action. In the course of a conversation, a person may say, "I've always dreamed of working from home." That's ripe fruit.

You won't even know it's hanging on the tree if you're talking too much, or if you're not listening carefully. And you'll leave it hanging on the tree if you don't know how to pick this wonderful fruit. For example, let's say you are listening when they share their dream of working from home. Most network marketers would launch into telling the person all about their great opportunity—talk, talk, talk. A better response, one that gets to the fruit, is to listen. Simply say, "So you've always dreamed of working from home. Can you tell me more about that." Or you might say, "What is it about working from home that's attractive to you?" Asking questions and listening enables the fruit to ripen on the vine before your eyes and ears, until finally, it nearly falls off on its own.

Stated most simply, telling isn't selling. I've been selling every day for fifteen years, and I've learned that the more I talk the less I sell. The more I listen, the better I sell. When I'm talking I'm not learning anything about my customers. What are their dreams? What are their goals? What are their secret desires? What would they do if they knew they couldn't fail? Where is their pain? How can I show them a way to heal their pain? By doing most of the talking, I will not discover these things about the person I'm trying to influence. In fact, I may be cheating someone out of the greatest opportunity of their life. The opportunity to be their own boss, work from home, make a positive difference, and get wealthy in the business of network marketing.

This book will show you a way toward mastery of listening—the most important skill for network marketing success. Why do I consider it the most important skill? Because no matter how successful you become, or how high you rise in your organization, you must build your business one person at a time. To do that, you must make a personal connection with people, a connection so powerful that it overcomes their natural resistance to change, to try something new, to leave their comfort zone. And the strongest link in the chain that connects people is the skill of listening.

You will learn how listening takes the pressure off you and the potential client or distributor. You will see why listening is the most powerful thing you can do when someone gives you a response such as, "But I don't like to sell," or "I don't want to sell to my friends." You will see why listening is the key to motivation. And you'll learn a proven model to dramatically improve your skill at listening.

Whether your network marketing company sells skin care, nutrition, weight loss, clean air and water, safety, financial services, travel, long-distance telephone service, utilities — it doesn't matter — we are all, first and foremost, in the people business. If you want to recruit, sponsor, and grow people, then you must master this skill of listening.

I learned (and am still learning) about listening the hard way. I began teaching listening skills in my seminars five years ago because I needed to learn to listen better. And teaching is one of the best ways to learn. Fifteen years of too many lost sales, relationships gone sour, a painful divorce, and eight years running my own sales training and consulting firm, have taught me an important lesson: poor listening leads to poor relationships and poor results. Simply put, the most successful and influential people in all walks of life tend to be the best listeners.

Network marketing success requires superior selling skills. Yet why is it that many people with little or no selling experience, and many who dread selling, have become super-successes in network marketing? You will read about Donna Larson-Johnson, a person who had no selling experience when she started her network marketing business. She was a full-time homemaker and mother who dreamed of creating a second income without having to leave her children at day-care. Today she's a leader in her company who has created wealth for herself and many other people with no selling experience.

Why is it that when you introduce people to your network marketing opportunity, so many reply, "But I don't like to sell!" Here is why. Most people believe that selling means *trying to convince someone to do something they don't want to do.* Who wants to do that for a living? You will rarely hear someone say, "Boy, I can't wait to get up today and see if I can get people to do something they don't want to do."

The people who have achieved greatness in this business know that sales is about something else entirely. They define it differently to themselves and to the people they sponsor and lead. Then they prove it with their actions. They know that sales is about helping people to make decisions which will add to the quality of their lives. Perhaps you could get excited about waking up to do that. Did you not join your network marketing company because you believed that it might help you to improve the quality of your life? Or did you join it because someone convinced you to do it, even though you didn't want to? If you did, you wouldn't be reading this book, because you would have already quit.

One of the great listeners in modern times was a man named Carl Rogers. Rogers was one of the most influential psychologists in American history. He founded the humanistic psychology movement, and revolutionized psychotherapy with his concept of client-centered therapy. If you were to study his work, you would see that client (customer)-centered therapy is all about listening. After 30 years of practice and research, Carl Rogers concluded that listening is the greatest tool we have for releasing human potential in others. If you want to grow your business, recruit and sponsor more quality people, and realize your life's dreams through the vehicle of network marketing, then read this book and practice what it preaches. You will become a better listener, and a better network marketer.

In chapter 1, you will learn why listening will make you different, more powerful, better liked, and wiser. In chapter 2, you will learn what it really means to listen and how listening opens the door to human motivation. Chapter 3 will show you why listening is so important, and why it's the most influential skill you possess. Chapter 4 will teach you what to listen for and pay attention to if you want to influence others. It will show you how to overcome the biggest waste of your precious time and tremendously increase your effectiveness. How to listen is the subject of chapter 5. You will learn the simple two-step formula and the advanced Multi-Level Listening™ formula. Good luck on your new adventure in the people business!

1

The Yearning

*"Give me the gift
of a listening heart."*
-King Solomon

THE WORLD IS YEARNING FOR PEOPLE with the courage and the desire to listen. Everyone you and I meet feels a deep longing to be heard. But who's listening? We pay therapists $100 per hour because we want the precious gift of someone's undivided attention.

People tend to listen better to customers, co-workers and bosses than to spouses, partners and children. A report I read stated that fathers spend an average of seven minutes per week listening to their children. Spouses spend about 26 minutes per week in meaningful conversation with one another.

Talking is a different matter all together. We live in a society of talkers. We've learned to believe that the most influential leaders, top salespeople, and brightest personalities are the best talkers. That's a false assumption. Think about it. Who most attracts you — people who talk too much or people who listen well? Would you rather follow a leader who always talks or one who listens and responds to you? Who would you rather buy from—a slick-talking salesperson or one who listens for your concerns, needs, wants and desires? What would you like most from your partner? Your boss? We all yearn for someone to listen, really listen to us.

Why is this? The great American psychologist, William James said, "The greatest need of the human soul is the need for appreciation, the need to feel important." Listening is how we know someone cares. We may care about someone, or say we care about them, but they'll never know it unless we listen to them.

When people know you care about them and their dreams, instead of only what you want from them, you tend to get what you want from them. You get what you want from others when you help them get what they want. If I want your participation in my downline, then I had better focus on what it will do for you, not what it will do for me.

Earlier I mentioned Donna Larson-Johnson, a highly successful network marketing leader. She joined her company for two reasons: she loved the skin care products, and she saw it as a way to stay at home with her children while creating a successful career. That was her dream, and she made it come true.

Donna learned the lesson of listening early in her network marketing career. One day she attempted to recruit someone by telling her that she could stay at home with her kids and have a successful business. After all, that is why Donna loved the business so much. She received only resistance in return. Donna persisted with this line of reasoning. Finally, the woman blurted out, "But I don't want to stay home with my kids. I need to get away before they drive me crazy! I saw this as an opportunity to put on beautiful clothes again, meet new people, and have conversations that go beyond goo-goo ga-ga."

This person, like all of us, yearned for someone to listen and understand her. By really listening, Donna began to understand what motivated her client. It gave Donna the opportunity to show her client how she could get what she wanted. That's what people want —someone who will care enough to listen and to share ideas that will improve the quality of *their* lives. Donna now asks this question. "Mary, if you were to do this business, what is it about what I do that is most attractive to you?"

Are you listening to people? Or are you waiting for your turn to talk? Do you take the time to really understand their world, to see it through their eyes? Or do you look for someone to hear your story? If you consistently and progressively make a shift from talking less to listening more, you will experience a shift in your business and relationships that will astound you. So read on, and find out how to use your unique human ability to listen and understand people.

Chapter 2

What Is Listening?

"Listening is wanting to hear."
-Jim Cathcart

O LISTEN IS TO CARE. People who care, listen. People who listen, care. Listening is also an act of love, because while love may be a feeling, it's also an activity. And a primary activity of love is listening.

Listening is also a path to enlightenment. We must temporarily suspend our judgments, and allow ourselves to be fully present for the other person. Buddhists call this state "mindfulness." Achieving this state of mind is one of our greatest human challenges. Imagine what would happen if we developed our capacity to listen to *ourselves,* to *others,* and to *God.* These are the three macro-levels of the Multi-Level Listening™ model. I wonder what my life would be like if I listened to that still, small voice within, more often. What if I listened to my own advice? What if I listened to the advice I gave others and applied it to my life? This is the art of listening to oneself. What if I listened to others so deeply that they felt loved, accepted, and safe in my presence, no matter what they had to say? And what if I listened to God, who speaks in so many ways that seem so hard to hear? When enough people learn to listen to self, others, and God, we will be moving toward a time of peace and enlightenment in our families, our nation and the world.

Listening is the key that opens the door to human motivation. *You cannot motivate someone to do something they don't want to do.* "A person convinced against his will is of the same opinion still." You can force them to do it. You can coerce them to do it. You can pay them to do it. But when you quit forcing, coercing, or paying, it's all over. People are motivated to do things they want to do. Motivation dwells within. It is human nature to move away from things that hurt and toward things that feel good. We want to move away from the things that detract from the quality of life and toward things that add to the quality of life. When you find out what those things are, for that person, you have the key to what motivates them.

We cannot find this out if we're talking. No matter how persuasive we are, we cannot convince someone to do something they don't want to do. No matter how many good reasons we give them — financial freedom! free time! vacations! be your own boss! — they are still our reasons, not theirs. Probably the greatest weakness among hundreds of network marketers I've observed, is that they *talk too much*. If we're talking, we're not learning anything. If we're talking, we don't know anything about the other person. We don't know what they want, what they need, where they hurt, what's important to them. I can only know what's important to me. And they know what's important to me too. By talking too much, I am proving what's most important to me—to recruit them—whether they like it or not! Remember this: *A person recruited against their will is a person unrecruited still.*

What if someone said to you, "But I don't want to sell to my friends." What would you say? Write it down. Go ahead.

_____

_____

_____

_____

Most people respond by trying to explain away the prospect's concern.

Distributor: "Oh, well you won't have to sell to your friends. It's just like recommending a movie or a restaurant. If you want them to see it, you'll tell them about it. That's what this is like."

Prospect: "Yeah, but they don't have to give me any money."

Distributor: "Well, most of your business won't come from your friends anyway, so you won't have to sell to them."

Prospect: "Who will I sell to?"

Distributor: "People you don't know. People you do business with, like your hairdresser. Or people you meet at parties and business meetings."

Prospect: "But I don't like to sell."

What's happening in this familiar conversation? It's conversational ping-pong. They are on opposite sides of the table, each person trying to win. The prospect digs in his or her heels. The distributor comes on stronger. No real communication takes place because the distributor does not understand the prospect. Why? Because she's talking instead of listening. Let's try it again, only this time I'll make the distributor a better listener.

Prospect: "But I don't want to sell to my friends."

Distributor: (pause) "It's interesting that you would say that. One of my most successful distributors also said that to me. Can you tell me more?"

Prospect: "Well, it's just that I can't stand it when people try to pressure me into doing something, so I don't want to pressure people either. I'm just not a salesperson."

Distributor: "So, you don't want to feel as if you're pressuring people, your friends or anyone else."

Prospect (feeling understood): "Yeah, I guess that's it."

Distributor: "When you think of the word "salesperson," you think about high-pressure, and that's just not you."

Prospect: "Right."

Distributor: "You know what? Just about everybody feels the way you do, because we've all had to deal with high-pressure salespeople. Even the people achieving wealth in our company feel that way."

Prospect: "They do? Well then how do they do it?"

Distributor: "Well, our company has developed ways to help people without using pressure. Would you be open to looking at it so you can judge for yourself?"

Do you see what happened in this example? By making one small but significant change in the way she responded to the prospect, the entire conversation went down a different track. It was cooperative, not competitive. It was helpful, not harmful. It moved forward instead of backward. What was that one difference? She listened.

Does this mean that listening will enable you to change every person's mind from no to yes? Of course not. It means that it's your best shot at presenting your idea to someone in a positive light. It's your best shot at getting a yes. If there were any guarantees on getting a yes, I'd write a book about that. Some people will have closed minds and that's all there is to it. Let them go. Don't waste your time or theirs. Others sit on the fence. They're not sure. They might convince themselves if they learn more. You can recruit skeptics, and they often become your best distributors. Don't lose them by talking too much. You increase the odds of winning them over by approaching them with a listening heart.

In Chapter 5, *How To Listen*, you will see that the distributor in the previous example followed a simple listening model. Notice I didn't say *easy*. The model is simple, but not easy. If listening were easy, or natural, everyone would be doing it. Listening is hard work.

What Listening Is Not

Listening is not...

+ half-listening because good, kind, or nice people do.
+ half-listening because you don't know how to get away without hurting or offending someone.
+ pretending you're interested when you're not.

+ looking for the weak points in an argument so you can always be right, listening to get ammunition for attack.

+ looking for one specific piece of information at the expense of everything else.

+ preparing your next comment while the other person is talking.

+ sitting still with your mouth shut (a corpse can do that).

+ being passive (listening is an active process).

+ waiting for your turn to talk.

Listening is not the same as hearing. Hearing is a physiological process. Listening is a mental and emotional process. Author M. Scott Peck writes that he once listened so hard to understand a speaker that he began to sweat. That is wanting to hear.

One of the best listeners I know happens to be deaf. Because he cannot hear with his ears, he focuses his full attention on the speaker's body language, facial expressions, and lips. He asks questions to gain clarity, and his responses come only after carefully considering what the speaker has communicated. He's a great listener because he *wants* to listen.

You may not need to sweat to listen well, but to apply the listening skills you learn in this book, you'll need to work at it and practice, practice, practice. I can guarantee you that the enormous payoff will make it worth the effort. With practice, it will become natural to you. People will be even more attracted to you. They will tell you what a great listener you are. And they'll begin listening to you, too.

Chapter 3

Why Listen?

"If you love to listen, you will gain knowledge and if you incline your ear, you will become wise."

-Sirach

THE DISTRIBUTOR IN THE PREVIOUS EXAMPLE gained understanding, trust, and rapport. She learned about the other person's true concerns. She discovered that "selling to her friends" was not the prospect's real underlying fear. Her fear was that she would need to become a high-pressure salesperson. She learned because she listened.

In the first example, the distributor proved that her prospect was right to be concerned about high-pressure selling. By trying to convince her that she shouldn't worry about selling to her friends, the distributor behaved like a high-pressure salesperson. Not only that, she didn't even respond to the prospect's real concern. In the second example she showed her that there is a better way. Listening is the opposite of pressure. Listening leads to success. Listening is the fuel of progress in the network marketing business. Pressure is like a brake on the wheels of progress.

So why is it a good idea to become a better listener? The short answer is that we often get ourselves into trouble by not listening. Not listening causes pain in our personal and professional relationships — conflicts, misunderstandings, arguments, lost business, and hurt feelings—much of which we can avoid by listening. The quality of our relationships determines the quality of our lives. Poor quality relationships lead to a poor quality of life. High quality relationships lead to a high quality of life. When you think about the most painful moments of your life, they most likely involved some kind of conflict with another person. And when you remember the happiest moments of your life, they most likely involved an experience with another person.

I can think of many times in my life that I wish I had listened better. I can remember frustrating conversations that occurred when I cared only about my agenda, when my ego felt threatened, or when I became too stubborn to hear what another person had to say. Every time that has happened, I've regretted it. I can also remember times when I didn't feel like listening, but I did it anyway. Every time that has happened, I've been grateful. I've discovered that the first step to effective listening is to become quiet. I've learned that sometimes it's better to walk away from a conversation until I can return with a listening heart.

We tend to listen least when we need to listen most. When the heat of emotions is pushing our buttons and pulling our triggers—that is when we most need to listen. It is also when listening becomes the most difficult! Anger, frustration, and disappointment become like "emotional cotton" in our ears.

I remember a day several years ago, when I was relaxing at home with my fiancé. She got up to get the mail and the next thing I know she's shoving a letter in my face and yelling, "What's this?!!"

I yelled back, "It's a letter. What's your problem?!!"

"Who is this woman?" she screamed. "I want to know who this woman is!"

I looked at the envelope and saw that it was from one of my clients. My immediate reaction was to scream at her for attacking me. I wanted to throw it back in her face, and yell, "It's from my client, Susan Smith! Get off my back!" Then I would stomp away with righteous indignation, feeling the adrenaline rush of rightness—but not feeling very happy at all.

By an act of grace I was struck with a flash of insight. I realized I needed to listen, or this would escalate into a frustrating battle. I realized that I should practice what I preach about listening. I wanted to "react" with anger, because *I felt angry* for being attacked. Instead, I paused and took a couple of deep breaths (it's impossible to talk while you're taking slow, deep breaths). Then I looked at her and said,

"You sound really upset."

"You're damn right I'm upset!"

"I'm sorry you're so upset, and I'd really like to understand what you're upset about." This response caught her completely off guard.

"I just don't like it," she said, still upset but getting calmer.

I paused and looked at her for a few seconds, thinking about what she said. "Will you tell me what it is you don't like, so I can understand?"

"Well, you travel so much on business. You stay in nice hotels, and you're up speaking in front of all those people. You meet a lot of women, and I don't know who they are or what you're doing."

"Oh. I see. It sounds like not knowing frustrates you."

"It does. It makes me feel insecure."

(Pause). "It sounds like your worried about me meeting other women when I'm away."

"I want to trust you and trust our relationship more."

"You know, if I were in your shoes, I might feel the same way. Can we talk about it?"

And so we did. Does that mean the problem was automatically resolved? Of course not. What it means is that it has the *possibility* of getting resolved. Without listening, human relations problems are rarely solved. Instead, negative feelings get buried, and feelings buried alive, live. Then they fester and grow like a cancer, killing intimacy, understanding, and joy.

That day I discovered once again that I can learn a lot by listening. If I had reacted the way I felt in the moment, what might have happened? Escalating frustration and anger would have led to little understanding of the real issue. When we listen we not only help ourselves to understand, we help the people we interact with to better understand themselves.

Carl Rogers describes this kind of listening in his book, *On Becoming A Person*. He writes,

"[Listening] is the most powerful force we know for altering the basic personality structure of an individual and improving his relationships and his communication with others. If I can listen to what he can tell me, if I can understand how it seems to him, if I can see its personal meaning for him, if I can sense the emotional flavor it has for him, then I will be releasing potent forces of change in him."

Here is an exercise Carl Rogers recommends if you want to do two things: improve your relationship with someone you care about and find out how hard it is to really listen.

"The next time you get into an argument with someone, stop the discussion for a moment, and for an experiment, institute this rule. Each person can speak up for him or her self only after she has first restated the ideas and feelings of the other speaker accurately, and to that speaker's satisfaction."

You will probably discover that this is one of the most difficult things you have ever tried to do. It takes courage because to understand a person this deeply, to permit ourselves to enter her private world and see the way life appears to her, is to run the risk of being changed. And to most of us, the risk of being changed is a truly frightening prospect.

But there is no growth without change. To change is to grow. If we want to grow personally and professionally, if we want to build better relationships, become more effective at involving people in our network marketing company, and grow our organizations, then we must learn to listen a little bit better each day.

What to Listen For

*"Wisdom is the reward you get
for a lifetime of listening when
you'd rather have been talking."*
-Aristotle

When my fiancé confronted me with the letter, my natural response was to defend myself. But doing what felt *natural* instead of *wise* would have led to a frustrating and fruitless argument. Fortunately, in this instance, I did what at first felt unnatural. I listened. And by listening, I realized that her real concern lay deeper, that I needed to find out more. If I had only listened to the surface level of her communication, I would have missed what really mattered to her.

Listen for the message behind the message

To listen effectively, we need to listen to more than the *presenting message*. The presenting message is communicated with words. But words are only part of communication. The real message often runs deeper, beneath the words. When emotions are involved, most of the meaning in a person's message lies under the waterline. So listening only to the words is like seeing the tip of an iceberg and believing we've seen the whole thing. Ninety percent of the iceberg lies under the water and ninety percent of the meaning in communication lies hidden beneath the words. Multi-Level Listening™ requires that we listen to more than the message. We listen not only to the words, but the space between the words. We listen not only to the *lyrics*, but to the *music*. We listen not only for the *content* of the message, but for the *intent* as well. Effective listening requires us to understand the message behind the message.

After one of my presentations on effective listening, a network marketing leader named Sandra Tillinghast told me the following story. A distributor in her downline named "Carol" had a talent for pushing Sandra's buttons. Nearly every time she called, Carol would complain to Sandra that she wasn't doing enough to help her. She would accuse Sandra of not supporting her, and of making her life difficult. Then she would tell Sandra how she needed to fix her problems. Sandra told me, "As soon as she started in on me I would shut down, and I didn't hear what she said after that. I would react defensively, and we never got anywhere. It became very frustrating, and this relationship took too much of my time and emotional energy. I actually began to doubt myself and feel resentful towards her. Now I know that if I had used your listening formula, I could have discovered what she was really saying. After many months of repeating these unproductive conversations, I finally realized that underneath her words she was trying to tell me that she was afraid and didn't know what to do next. That was the message behind the message. If I had listened better, I could have responded to her real concerns and saved both of us a lot of anguish."

Remember, before you can respond effectively you need to get a handle on the message behind the message—what radio personality Paul Harvey calls "the story behind the story." When someone is angry, what's behind the anger? When someone is sad, where does the sadness come from? When someone is joyful, what's behind that emotion? Understanding another person at this level is what human potential author Ken Keyes called "the instant consciousness doubler." When we see things from another person's point-of-view, we have doubled our consciousness because we now see twice as much as we did before.

Persistence, not insistence, is the key to persuasion. We cannot persuade someone by insisting that they see things our way. *We need to persist until we see things their way.* And we do that by asking questions and listening. Only then can we open the door to persuasion. Before we can take someone where we want them to go, we need to start with where they are. The best way I know to do this is to listen for the message behind the message.

Talking tends to push and listening tends to pull. Pushing tends to create *resistance*, and pulling tends to create *assistance*. Trying to convince someone by talking them into our way of seeing things is like pushing a wagon by its handle. The wagon goes every direction except the one we want it to go. Pull the wagon, and it follows. **Persistence, not insistence, overcomes resistance.**

Listen For Their Dreams

A popular phrase in many network marketing companies goes, "Sell The Dream!" A good idea, but the question is, whose dream? Listen to a distributor attempting to recruit someone by selling the dream. Notice how they enthusiastically tell the prospect how they can make their dreams comes true by joining their network marketing company. The problem with this approach is that the distributor doesn't even know the prospect's dreams! Why doesn't she? Because she hasn't asked. She is too busy talking.

Instead of selling the dream of your network marketing company, you need to discover the dream of your potential distributor. Find out what their dreams are, then show them a way to live out their dreams using your network marketing company as a vehicle.

For example, I am a professional speaker and trainer. That has always been my dream and now it's the way I make my living. I love to speak to groups and help the people in those groups to live better lives. Many network marketers have attempted to recruit me into their companies. They tell me how great their company is, what a great compensation plan they have, and how I can make a lot of money and be my own boss. Since I'm already my own boss and I make a lot of money now, I ask myself, "What's in it for me?" I love what I do, why would I want to become a network marketer? I wouldn't. . . unless they could find out that one of my dreams is to do what I do in an even bigger way. If they could show me how I could continue to do what I do, but do it in a bigger way by becoming involved with their company, I could be persuaded. But to do that they must first ask me questions about my dreams, then listen while I tell them.

To succeed in network marketing, we need to stop selling our dreams and find out the about the dreams of the person we're talking to instead. How do we do that? By asking questions and listening.

Listen for Success

If you were to lead a team that must survive in the jungle without supplies for one month, and you could choose who to bring, would you take just anyone who came along? Of course not. You would screen them carefully. After all, your life and the lives of your team-members depend on it. So if someone says, "Sign me up," be cautious. Why invest time and energy into someone who won't add value to your organization? Find out more about them first. Is this someone you would enjoy talking to frequently? Do you want to share dinners, car rides or your home with them? Do you trust this person? Do they have a track record of success or have they learned from failure?

To improve your skill at creating a winning organization, I recommend that you watch for three types of people: the **wise**, the **foolish**, and the **destructive**. Let me describe them to you.

Wise distributors

Wise people respond to the light of truth. When you tell them your truth, they listen. They think about it. They evaluate it reasonably and objectively. If it fits, they make changes. They have a desire to grow and learn. They know that seeing is better than being blind, even if it hurts. In essence, they are coachable. Wise people receive feedback with this attitude: "I will listen, take it all in. I can never be worse off by knowing more, even if I don't agree." Wise people chew the fruit and spit out the seeds.

Foolish distributors:

Foolish people reject the light. They don't want feedback. They don't accept coaching. They don't want to change and grow. They would rather experience the pain of staying the way the are than face the pain of changing. They trade short-term gain for long-term pain. Seeing hurts too much, so they would rather remain blind. Foolish people rarely even taste the fruit (maybe they'll take a bite or two). How many network marketers have wasted thousands of hours trying to turn a foolish person into a wise person? People can change, and they do change, but you can't change people.

Destructive distributors

Wicked people destroy the light. They are the grumblers and faultfinders. When they don't succeed they want to make sure that no one else does either. They're negative, they don't keep agreements, and they always have an excuse. Wicked people stomp on the fruit, hoping no one else will taste it either.

Listen to find out if you want this person on your team. Do you want to invest your most precious resources of time and energy into this person? If not, then move on. Does this person have dreams? If not, then move on. If they do, ask them questions and listen to discover their dreams. Then do them a favor. Show them how becoming involved in your network marketing company can help them realize their dreams.

Listening for success means that you listen because listening will make you more successful. It also means listening for clues that will tell you if others will be successful too.

Chapter 5

How to Listen

IRST, I WANT TO GIVE YOU the short model for effective listening. Master it first, then move on to the advanced model. The short model has two steps and it goes like this...

Ask! Listen!

That's it. Notice that talk is not in this formula. Most networkers use another two-step formula. It has two steps also, but it goes...

Talk! Talk More!

I recommend the first model. Ask with enthusiasm then listen with great attention. Here's another way to look at my two-step formula for listening...

Shut up and stop talking so much!

Where did we get the idea that it's our job to fix other people's problems? When did we begin to believe that we had to have an answer to help a friend in pain, when all they really want and need is someone to listen and understand?

I don't want you to have a simple and quick solution to my difficult problem. When you supply an instant solution you discredit the seriousness of my problem, and you therefore discredit me. You are sending the message that my problem is insignificant because all I have to do to solve it is take your advice.

During my seminars, women often relate the following scenario. "When I've had a bad day at work, or a problem with my boss, I want to tell my husband about it. I need someone to listen, so I can work out my frustration or anger. But as soon as I finish telling him what happened, he responds with an instant solution. He'll say, "Tomorrow, when you go to work, here's what you should do...". When he does that, I feel even more frustrated, so I call one of my friends and tell her about it. I feel so much better when I hear her say, "Gosh, it sounds like that really hurt you."

Rarely, when people share a concern or problem with us, do they want us to try to solve it for them. We yearn for someone to listen, to understand, and to care. *We need to stop answering and giving advice!* Forget being Mr. Fix-it or Miss Fix-it. Just listen.

We quickly discover how difficult this is to do. We must form a new, better habit. It's like giving up cigarettes and replacing them with vitamins. Talking too much is to relationships what cigarettes are to the body. Listening is to our relationships, what vitamins are to the body. One promotes dis-ease, and the other promotes health.

So before learning the Multi-Level Listening™ model, you need to first master the two-step formula. Why? Because the law of listening says, "You gotta wanna." Some people don't want to listen, so to teach listening skills to them is fruitless. I enjoy visiting the home of my friends—a couple with three kids. I enjoy them because they're fun, good-hearted people. I also notice that they haven't heard anything I've said all evening. They haven't heard anything that anyone else says either. Nobody listens to anybody around their house. I could teach them all the listening skills in the world, but if they don't want to listen to each other, learning new skills won't help them. The moral is, first, you gotta wanna.

The Multi-Level Listening Model

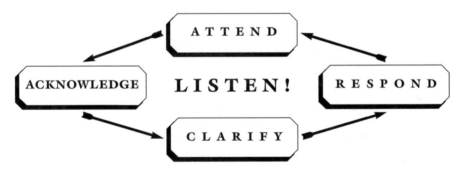

Paying Attention

The first key to effective listening is to attend. Attend means to pay attention, and this is perhaps the most difficult step to effective listening. Paying attention is difficult. It takes practice. It's difficult because our minds are so easily distracted.

Two types of distractions–external and internal–prevent us from paying attention to the speaker. External distractions include noises, other people, telephones, or something about the person we're listening to — the way they dress, or the way they talk, for example. Internal distractions make it even more difficult. Thinking about other things, thinking about what we're going to say next, jumping to conclusions, mind-reading, and making assumptions about the speaker's meaning, all get in the way of true communication.

Multi-Level Listening™ requires intense attention. If you have something on your mind that prohibits you from concentrating on the speaker, see if you can call a time out. Tell the speaker that now is not a good time because you are preoccupied and you want to listen later when you can give them the attention they deserve. This is always better than trying to fake listening. You cannot fake listening.

To give the gift of listening we must train ourselves to let go of distractions and to pay attention. We must be present. We need to care enough to slow down and get ourselves out of the way. We need to care enough to pause.

I have found that the more I practice this, the better I get. I have also found that it has a powerful effect on the other people. They begin to open up and to share more of themselves. New levels of trust and rapport develop. It makes them feel important.

Do this one thing the next time someone talks to you: pay attention. Attend. Then attend some more. Practice and never stop practicing. You will get better, and it will transform your communication.

Acknowledging You've Paid Attention

The next key is to *acknowledge*. When you acknowledge what the other person has said it shows concern and respect for the speaker. It will prove that you are a responsive and caring person. Another word for acknowledge is *empathize*. We empathize with the speaker by acknowledging their position. It doesn't necessarily mean we *agree* with them. It does mean we are attempting to *understand* them. We are beginning to understand the speaker's meaning and feelings behind the meaning. Acknowledging reduces friction and resistance and helps to create a climate of trust and rapport.

At first, this step may seem easy. It is simple, but it is not easy. When I teach listening skills, it often takes up to two hours for people to put it into practice. Please do not underrate this step. Think about it. Visualize yourself doing it. Then try it right away.

There are many ways to acknowledge the speaker. One of the best is simply to *pause* when the speaker has finished. Remember, in communication it's the little things that make the big difference.

You may have noticed that most people begin talking right away, sometimes before the last word has left your lips. And sometimes they interrupt you. What message does this send? It says that they haven't listened to you. They've been formulating their response while you were talking. So just pause, and look the person in the eye. Pause for two to four seconds. I call this the Golden Silence. What message does this send? It says, "What you've said is important enough for me to reflect upon before I respond. I have listened, and now I'm considering what you mean."

Pausing often feels uncomfortable at first. We're not used to silence in communication. A great way to pause is simply to take a deep breath. It's impossible to talk and take a deep breath at the same time.

Another method is to give the speaker what I call verbal pauses. When they finish speaking, simply say, "I see," or "Oh," or "Ahh, or "Umm." This one little step can transform the communication process. Why? Because it proves to the speaker that you are listening. It forces you to slow down and pay attention. It feels good to you and to the speaker. It will help you to share meaning and gain understanding. Try it! Don't overlook this step. Just try it out ten times and decide for yourself if it works for you.

As you improve your skill, try acknowledging the emotional message that the person is sending. This is more challenging. But if you want someone to feel truly understood, then you must listen for and acknowledge their feelings. Here are some examples:

"It sounds like you're really upset about this."

"I sense some hesitation in your response."

"You must feel hurt by that."

"You're raising an important issue."

"I'm glad you brought this up."

"It must hurt to be treated that way."

"You've had other experiences with network marketing that make you leery."

"I see. You feel like to make it in network marketing, you'll have to pressure people."

"I understand. You feel that selling doesn't fit your personality."

"It looks like you're feeling unsure about this."

"You're angry about what happened with another company."

For another example, let's look at the story I told earlier — the one where my fiancé yelled and my initial reaction was defensive. Let's see what might have happened if I had followed my initial reaction.

"What's this?!!"

"It's a letter," I yelled back, "What's your problem?!!"

"Who is this woman?" she screamed. "I want to know who this woman is!"

"It's from my client, Susan Smith! Get off my back!"

What do you notice about this conversation? Did I acknowledge her? No, I did not. First of all, I didn't pause. I just reacted. She yelled and I yelled right back. That's useless. The smart thing to do, what mature communicators do, is to acknowledge the emotional message. I could do that by saying,

"What's this?!!!"

(Pause, breathe!) "Wow. It sounds like you're really frustrated."

At this point, she is likely to respond in one of two ways. If my perception is on track, she might say, "You're damn right I'm frustrated!" On the other hand, if my perception is off-track, she might respond with, "No, I'm not frustrated, I'm angry!"

It doesn't really matter if I'm right or not. The point is that I am acknowledging what I perceive. This gives the speaker the chance to affirm or correct my perception. Either way, it begins the process of defusing friction, tension, and resistance.

Sometimes the speaker won't calm down right away. It might take two or three acknowledges before she realizes that someone is actually listening. Some people get so shocked by this realization that they forget what upset them in the first place! Listening transforms the communication process.

Getting Clear

To give the prospect an intelligent and effective response, we must first clarify what he or she means. To clarify means: to make transparent, unclouded, distinct, sharp. It means to illuminate. We clarify to get on the same wavelength and to gain a sense of shared meaning. The response we want when we clarify what the other person means is, "Yes, that's it!" or "You've got it!"

The biggest mistakes made in selling the network marketing opportunity stem from poor listening. When we fail to listen carefully, we often make costly yet avoidable errors. For example, what if someone says...

Prospect: "How long have you been in this business?"

Consultant: "Six months."

Prospect: "No thanks. I'm not interested."

Look at the graphic of the Multi-Level Listening™ model. Of the four elements to the model, which one did the consultant jump to? Did she acknowledge? No. Did she clarify? No. She jumped right to respond. And that's what gets us into trouble! Jumping to a response before we've acknowledged and clarified often leads to frustrating communication problems. Let's try another example, this time using the acknowledge and clarify elements.

Prospect: "How long have you been in this business?"

Consultant: "That's an interesting question (acknowledge). Can you tell me why that's important to you? (clarify)

Prospect: "Well, I don't want to get involved in something that's unproved."

Consultant: "I see. (acknowledge) You're only interested in opportunities that have a proven track record. (clarify)

Prospect: "That's right. I'm not the type for "ground floor" opportunities."

Consultant: "What would you like to see to be convinced that this is a proven opportunity?

Prospect: "Well, I'd like to meet five people who've been successful with your company for at least two years."

Consultant: "Great. I can do that. What other concerns do you have?"

You probably noticed that the prospect didn't really care how long that distributor had been in the business. In the first example, the distributor responded to the presenting message and by doing so, shot herself in the foot. In the second example, by acknowledging and clarifying, she listened for the message behind the message, discovered the prospect's true concern (a proven track record), and responded in a way that got positive results.

Another thing you may have noticed is that it takes a little more work. It takes asking intelligent questions, like a detective, a doctor, or a therapist might ask. I'll say it again, listening is hard work, but the payoff is worth it every time.

We clarify by asking open questions. Open questions are the key to effective listening. They prevent us from making stupid assumptions. Here are some examples of open questions:

+ "Tell me more."
+ "Can you tell me more?"
+ "How do you mean?"
+ "Can you tell me more about your concern?"
+ "I'd like to understand before I respond. Can you elaborate?"
+ "I'd like to understand your frustration. What else is troubling you?"
+ "So, your concern is..."

Seeking clarity allows you to gain understanding, to see the world from the other person's point of view, to sense how it feels to her. If you can see the world through Joe Jones' eyes, you can sell Joe Jones what Joe Jones buys.

Here's another example, from the conversation in chapter 2.

Prospect: "But I don't want to sell to my friends."

Distributor: "I see. (acknowledge) It's interesting that you would say that. (acknowledge) One of my most successful distributors said that to me also. Can you tell me more?" (clarify)

Prospect: "Well, it's just that I can't stand it when people try to pressure me into doing something, so I wouldn't want to do that to people either. I'm just not a salesperson."

Distributor: "So, you don't want to feel like you're pressuring people, your friends or anyone else." (clarify)

Prospect (feeling understood): "Yeah, I guess that's it."

Distributor: "And when you think of the word "salesperson," you think about high-pressure, and that's just not for you."

Prospect: "You've got it."

Before we respond to the speaker's concern, we need to understand the concern. That's why we need to look beneath the surface with Multi-Level Listening™ skills. It gives us a better chance to respond in a way that respects the speaker, proves that we care, and greatly increases the probability that we can help them overcome their resistance to change. The goal is to get someone to consider, to look at the opportunity, so that they can make a fully informed decision.

I have asked many highly successful network marketers, "If you had it to do over again, what would you do differently?" Nine out of ten gave me the same response. "I would spend less time trying to convince people who aren't interested and more time working with people who are." I agree wholeheartedly. But my question is this: "How many more people may have been interested in the network marketing opportunity if it had been presented by someone who really listened?" Remember, telling isn't selling. We sell best by listening.

Ben Feldman, one of the greatest insurance salespersons of all time, had a two-step sales success formula. He said the first step is to find the problem. The second step is to create an idea to solve the problem. You can't find the problem unless you listen with all of your senses and all of your heart. That's what Multi-Level Listening™ is all about. You need to find out what to respond to, before you respond.

Giving the best information

Now it's time to respond. Remember, if you're not careful, you will go right from attend to respond. Responding too quickly is a tough habit to break. **Attend, acknowledge, clarify,** *then* **respond.** If you're a skeptic, don't believe what I'm saying. Go out and try it for yourself. You'll never know if you like sushi — or hate it — until you try it.

When we understand what a person means we can feel confident that we will give a better response. Realize that you don't always need to have an answer. We can never have all the answers, but we can always give a response.

Responding is the easy part when we've really listened. We can:

+ provide a solution or an answer, when it's appropriate
+ provide resources
+ agree to take action
+ invite them to a meeting
+ give them a sample
+ educate them
+ give them a tape, article, or book
+ suggest options and alternatives
+ suggest that the speaker find solutions
+ suggest that the speaker return with options
+ put the ball back in their court

   "What do you suggest?"

   "What do you plan to do about it?"

"This sounds like something you need to handle. I'll support you however I can."

If you can respond in 20 words, don't use 50. It's better to say too little than to say too much. When you say too little, if the other person is interested, they will ask for more. When you say too much, even if they are interested, you increase the odds of losing their interest. Never over-sell. I recently listened to a conversation between a customer and representative of a nutrition line. The customer asked a question about an herbal product and the salesperson answered her. She said, "Great, I'll take it." The salesperson then continued to sell it to her and the customer changed her mind!

When to use the model

The best time to use the Multi-Level Listening™ model is when you need it. When do you need it? More often than you might think. If someone says, "What's your name?", the model isn't needed. If someone asks, "When can I start?", you don't need to say, "That's an interesting question. Can you tell me more?" Or, if they say, "No way!", then don't use it. However, if there is any ambiguity in the person's question or statement; if you're unclear about anything they may have said; if any of the words they use could have two or more meanings; if there is any emotional content to the message, then the model will help you to listen more effectively.

Understand that meanings are in people, not in words. "Sometimes" might mean something much different to you than it does to the other person. The 500 most used words in the English language have over

14,000 definitions. Which one do they mean? What if they say, "I'm interested"? How interested are they? If someone says, "I don't like multi-level marketing," why do they say that? And what do they mean by multi-level marketing? If someone is unsure, or frustrated, or confused, or lacks confidence, they don't need us to talk them out of it by giving our brilliant advice. They need someone to listen and to understand.

A great time to use the Multi-Level Listening™ model is when you want to teach others to be great listeners. The best way to teach is to walk your talk. Modeling excellence is the essence of leadership.

My friend, Ted Tillinghast, is a "network marketing husband." He totally supports his wife, Sandra, in her business. Ted read the manuscript of this book and put the ideas to use right away, with great results. One evening, Sandra was holding an opportunity meeting at her house, but she had to leave on an emergency. People from her downline continued the meeting without her. By the time Ted got home from work, the meeting was almost over. Only one prospect remained, and she was surrounded by five distributors all telling her about the company. Ted noticed that everyone was talking except the prospect. So he stepped in, introduced himself, and began asking her questions and listening. The results were dramatic. This woman began to open up. Her posture changed from a defensive one to an open one. By continuing to ask her questions, Ted discovered what interested her about the opportunity. Within fifteen minutes, the woman became so excited that she asked to become a distributor. The next day, Ted played the messages on his answering machine for me. Three of the five distributors who saw this happen left messages. They were ecstatic about what had happened. By modeling the way, Ted had taught them the secret skill of network marketing success.

Use the Multi-Level Listening™ model when you want to understand someone or when you want them to understand you. When you listen first, it increases the chance that the other person will return the favor. Use it when you want to establish a strong common bond. It will ensure that you create the best chance to influence them. Use it when you want to reduce conflict, increase your persuasiveness, and when you want to get what you want by helping others get what they want.

Chapter 6

Final Thoughts

THE TWO-STEP LISTENING FORMULA is the simplest and most effective sales model in existence. Ask! Listen! Ask! Listen! Ask! Listen! It is a formula for success in the people business. Most salespeople use another formula. Talk! Talk More! Talk! Talk More! It is a formula for failure.

Listening is how we find out what motivates a person to take action. You and I can't motivate people. They must motivate themselves. When you light a fire under a snail, you get escargot. But when you light a fire under a person's dreams, you get action. Listen for what motivates them, and then give it to them.

Listening is the most effective way to sell. Why? Because people buy for their reasons, not yours. Stop giving them your reasons and listen for theirs instead.

Listening is how you take pressure out of the selling process. If you want to prove to people that they don't have to pressure people, then you must sell to them without pressuring them. If they feel better because they talked with you, then they may walk away thinking, "I'd like to do that."

Most people believe that selling is about trying to get people to do something they don't want to do. If you sell by talking too much, they're right. **True selling is about helping people to make decisions that will add to the quality of their lives.** And you can only do that if you listen.

Another Final Note

I'd love to hear your listening stories. Please call, write, e-mail or fax them to me.

I also teach listening and selling skills to network marketing companies and other sales organizations, so please invite me or refer me to someone. If you do, I'll provide you with a gift of my audiocassette program called, *Mental Muscle–Seven Principles for Strengthening Your Sales.*

Steve Shapiro

P.O. Box 1047

Laguna Beach, CA 92652

phone: 949-494-8715

fax: 949-376-5971

e-mail: steveshapiro@mindspring.com

About the Author

If you want to get pumped up for a few hours, then listen to a motivational speaker. If you want to get business and personal results, then listen to Steve Shapiro.

Two things make Steve Shapiro's speeches and seminars different from the rest:

1. You get ultra-high levels of customization that address your company's unique situation and products. Steve has never given the same presentation twice.

2. You get business results you can measure, not just high marks on the evaluations.

"After six years of successfully entertaining and motivating my audiences, like all the other speakers, I realized that a month later nothing had changed. People remember that they liked the presentation, and they might remember a story, but they weren't changing their behavior or their results. So two years ago, *I* changed. Now instead of trying to motivate people by pumping them up, I give them very specific things they can do right away to get better results in their lives and their business. And guess what? That's when they started to get really motivated in a whole new way."

Steve started his own home-based business eight years ago, and now owns a successful speaking, training, and consulting firm called Shapiro Resource Group. He's the author of three books, a five-part video series and an audiocassette program called *Mental Muscle —Seven Principles for Strengthening Your Sales.* His clients include network marketing companies, entrepreneurial start-ups and Fortune 1000 companies, including American Express, Compaq, Yamaha and Marriott.

Listening *for* Success

How to Master the Most Important Skill of Network Marketing

Additional copies of this book may be purchased at the following volume discounts...

	Quantity	S Total
❏　1 to　9 copies at $9.95 each	_____	_____
❏　10 to 49 copies at $8.95 each	_____	_____
❏　50+ copies at $6.95 each	_____	_____
Over 250 copies, call for Volume Price		

Shipping & Handling: $3.00 for 1st book, 50¢ each additional book

Name: _____

Organization: _____

Phone: _____

Street Address: _____

P.O. Box: _____

City, State, Zip: _____

Country: _____

Purchase Order Number *(if applicable)*: _____

❏ Check Enclosed

❏ Visa　❏ MasterCard　❏ American Express　❏ Discover

Account Number: _____ Exp. Date: _____

Signature: _____

Applicable sales tax, shipping and handling charges will be added. Prices subject to change.

> **Orders may be faxed to: (888) 883-8128**
> **or call our toll free number: (800) 533-2885**
> **or drop your order in the mail using this form.**

BLUE RIBBON VIDEO

3405 W. Nob Hill Boulevard ✦ Yakima, Washington 98902

www.blueribbonvideo.com

Free Video

Steve Shapiro is an excellent speaker who would enjoy making a presentation at your event. Call Blue Ribbon video at 1-800-533-2885 to request a video featuring Steve's presentation. You'll be able to see the impact he has on the audience and will agree that his message will make a positive difference in the lives of those who attend. Then give us a call to schedule him to speak.

Source for Network Marketing Sales Tools

Blue Ribbon is a low cost source for prospecting and training/motivational tapes and books for Network Marketers. Visit our website at www.blueribbonvideo.com or call us at 1-800-533-2885 to check our prices.

Here are some examples of our many products:

For Nikken Distributors:

- NIKKEN BUSINESS REVIEW – Very popular and attractive single sheet introduction to Nikken
- DENNIS AND RUTH WILLIAMS STORY AND OPPORTUNITY video – Over 100,000 sold
- MAGNETIC FIELD APPLICATION HANDBOOK

For All Network Marketers:

- *Dare to Dream and Work to Win* by Tom Barrett
- *Being the Best You Can Be in MLM* by John Kalench
- *Who Stole the American Dream?* by Burke Hedges
- *You Were Born Rich* by Bob Proctor

Comments from Nikken Leaders...

"Listening is the key to success in Nikken. Leaders are seasoned listeners. I've wanted to have this book to offer my organization many times. Thank you Steve for writing it. This book is a must for serious people builders. Nikken is more than building a business. It's about building people and people build the business. When we listen we come in contact with people's heart and their heartbeat. Listening to their heartbeat then directs us in leading them to their desired outcome."

Marlene Eborn
Nikken Royal Diamond Distributor

"Our success in life is directly proportional to the quality of our relationship with others. Read this book. It will make a difference in your life and deepen your relationship with others."

Dave Johnson
Nikken Royal Diamond Distributor

"I love Steve Shapiro's 2-step technique: ask, then listen! Such simple advice, yet so profound! Steve's book *Listening for Success* is full of wisdom, humility, and humor. These ideas, when applied daily in our lives, have the power to transform our personal and business lives."

Trish Schwenkler
Nikken Royal Diamond Distributor

"There is nothing more vital to one's success in this business than the ability to listen. The revered masters of network marketing have taken the skill of listening from a simple discipline to a true art form. Steve's powerful little book teaches you how to walk in the steps of the masters."

John Kalench
Founder of Millionaires in Motion
Nikken Diamond Distributor

"We realize that it's imperative to improve on our listening skills in life and especially in our filed of network marketing. Steve Shapiro has hit the all time grand slam with *Listening For Success*. We have added it to our must read list for starting your Nikken business."

William and Jan Todd
Nikken Diamond Distributors

"One of our greatest challenges has been developing enough respect for other individuals. Listening to others will help us define their reality and show our respect. Now that Nikken has provided us with a vehicle for the creation of a new way of life we can facilitate other peoples' development. Listening is a willingness to risk-a willingess to love. If we listen we can keep hope alive and elevate ourselves to a higher state. The higher up we go-the more gently down we reach."

Dr. Roger Boger
Nikken Royal Diamond Distributor

"Listening makes you a superstar and Steve Shapiro teaches you how to listen."

Mark Victor Hansen
Co-Author, Chicken Soup for the Soul

"This quick read packs more punch per page than any other book we know of."

Upline Journal

"This book is a great resource for improving your listening skills, which is a great resource for building a better business. Steve did it right."

Randy Gage
Gage Direct

"Thank you so much for a great presentation on listening at the Nikken Expo yesterday. My husband and I have just been introduced to Nikken and were exploring the company. The quality of your presentation tipped the balance and we signed the forms to become Nikken distributors before we left the Hilton. Thank you again for ideas that will help us both in many areas of our lives.

Margaret Cooker, RN
New Nikken Distributor